Food Ninjas

How to Raise Kids to Be Lean, Mean Eating Machines

BY MATT STONE

A proud presentation of:

September 2013
Copyright © 2013 180DegreeHealth, LLC. All rights reserved worldwide.
ISBN 1492933864
ISBN-13: 978-1492933861

DISCLAIMER

The material provided here is for educational and informational purposes only and is not intended as medical advice. The information contained in this book should not be used to diagnose or treat any illness, metabolic disorder, disease, or health problem. If you have developed a serious illness of some kind, the complexities of dealing with that disorder are best handled by your physician or other professional health care provider, whom you should also consult with before beginning any nutrition or exercise program. Use of the programs, advice, and other information contained in this book is at the sole choice and risk of the reader.

To Emily, the most badass little food ninja I know. May you always have the power to put a cookie down after only one bite—yet, at the same time have the power to eat your bodyweight in "fattening" food without gaining an ounce. You remind me of how unfortunate people who no longer eat according to their instincts really are.

May this book prevent more self-starved food neurotics from coming into being. It's much easier to start life with a healthy relationship with food than it is to rediscover normal eating after you've been through the magic diet circus.
~Matt Stone; August 2013

6

Contents

Introduction   9

Level 1: Strong Metabolism
Make Strong Ninja   15

Level 2: Ninja Need Special
Ninja Milk   29

Level 3: Ninja is not Mr.
Sailor Man   35

Level 4: Ninja is not Fish   55

Level 5: Ninja Training   60

Conclusion   70

References   74

Introduction

Now I know that you really wanted to raise a kid that would turn her nose at all that crappy modern food and just sit down to an organic peach while her friends ate birthday cake. That is like the definition of cool! I mean, who wants a kid that can just mindlessly ENJOY her childhood, enjoy hanging out with friends and not even think about every bite of food like you do?

Ughh, it just makes me cringe to think that someone could grow up in today's totally toxic day and age and not analyze every meal. To not know that the glycemic index of potatoes is higher than carrots? To not know the difference between sugars and complex carbs? To not read labels? To order what you FEEL like eating instead of what you know is the right choice? It disgusts me to think of how our children these days just eat like animals with no regard for fiber, lignans, fat soluble vitamin RDA's, or even cholesterol content (I mean some kids don't even know that the yolk, not the white, is where all the cholesterol is—can you imagine??!! It's a wonder they even survive childhood!).

Well, on the off chance that you don't want your kid to turn out like you, obsessing over every last detail of nutritional minutiae as if it somehow holds the key to the fountain of youth, worrying about whether or not mom's Christmas dinner will contain genetically-modified corn, longing for unhealthy foods, ballooning up 10 pounds every time you sniff a cookie, and living a pretty joyless food existence… You may have actually found the right book.

Every parent wants their kid to be as healthy as possible. I understand that. But there is more to consider here than just "nutritional science." We are complex, dynamic, socially-interactive modern human beings. For anyone, such as your child, to live the most complete and well-rounded life possible, many other factors must be taken into consideration. That's what *Food Ninjas* is all about. It's not just about the "perfect diet for your child," whatever that is. It's about navigating, even mastering, the modern food and lifestyle in a way that yields exceptional health and vitality.

The true Food Ninja in today's day and age doesn't lock him or herself away from society to avoid "bad" foods. She can have a big bag of cookies in the cupboard and think about something other than those cookies. In fact, those cookies might go stale and get thrown out. On other occasions one single cookie is all it takes. Just a little nibble or two and the cookies get peacefully placed back in the cupboard. Tasting a cookie doesn't lead to engulfing the entire bag and a major stomachache. On other occasions, ripping through a dozen cookies after a half of a pizza sounds like just what the doctor ordered. And so that's exactly what happens. And body fat levels stay exactly rock solid and unchanged from week to week, month to month, and year to year, whether it's one cookie or twenty, or whether the cookie fest came pre or post-workout. In the end, it all leads to a perfect balance over time without any conscious attempt to interfere with instinct.

Balance. That's a good word.

Is it balanced for your kid to eat an African tribal diet of root vegetables, fruit, chicken gizzards, and green vegetables for weeks on end, go to a friend's house, and then ignore all the other kids while engulfing enough Doritos and visible-from-outer-space glowing candies to reach the point of nearly vomiting? Is that really preparing your kid for a healthy co-existence with the modern food environment? Or do you want a kid who could live in a giant gingerbread house across the street from McDonald's and hardly think about food? Maybe even grab a banana to snack on when there are bowls of chocolate candies laid out all across the room?

Anyway, no need to get too carried away here in the introduction. For now, let's just say that when you look at the whole picture of health at any age and what constitutes a good life, raising a kid on some puritanical diet that you've read is the "optimal way to eat," sheltered from the rest of the world, not allowing the kid to eat a long list of items, limiting him or her to set amounts of "naughty" foods, forcing the kid to eat healthy foods for a "reward" like ice cream… Well, those just aren't the answers. That's a good way to get a kid sick, make him overly paranoid about what he eats, and initiate disordered eating behavior.

The premise of this book is that a healthy, happy life for your kids, and a healthy, happy relationship with food, is a lot closer than you think. It doesn't require extremism. In fact, you don't have to really teach your kid much of anything about what and how to eat. The kid's already fully programmed with all the tools required. You just need to shut up and get your stupid brain out of the way.

Much of what is said here is true for adults, too. Trying to eat a healthy diet and intellectualizing food choices—using your head to decide what and what not to eat at any given moment, is a huge problem that typically ends in abysmal failure for many reasons. The biggest problem is perhaps the distortion of hunger and fullness cues when one tries to consciously interfere with instinctual programming, as well as the message it sends your metabolism when you constantly deny yourself of what your internal cues are trying to drive you to eat. It sends the signal of *scarcity*, and if you don't think the body is programmed to know what scarcity is and respond accordingly to it, you're not giving your body nearly enough credit.

The intricacy of the feedback mechanisms we possess to regulate a wide array of physical functions in harmonious balance is truly astounding. Just dim the lights and your eyes completely change in a few seconds. But you don't think your kid's body can regulate food intake? Fluid intake? Energy expenditure? Body fat levels? Those were just optional features that your kid didn't come hardwired with? Come on now.

It's true that there are some things, aside from our conscious interference, that have the ability to interfere with our body's energy-regulating system. We will discuss those in this book a little. But ultimately our bodies work best when they dictate their own energy intake, without any conscious thought. If anything, your job as a parent is to protect that proper functionality, not force kids to eat vegetables, teach them horrifying things about foods that they like, and flip on the tube after dinner to watch an extreme weight loss television program with them. That's only going to pollute a kid's mind with thought for food, and thought for food leads to interference with instinct and a hard, lifelong, neurotic battle to try to figure out what, when, and how much to eat (when it otherwise could be effortless).

So let's begin training. If you are going to produce a Food Ninja—the kind that can throw away a half-eaten cookie like it's a throwing star, say no to junk food at a friend's house like it's been poisoned, yet at the same time eat like a Sumo wrestler on occasion, turning all that food into heat, muscle, and energy instead of layers of flab, you are going to have to be a worthy sensei. Sensei is supposed to mean like, teacher, for those of you who have spent the last three decades in a coma and have never seen a *Karate Kid* movie.

So get ready. Do some stretches or something.

Level 1: Strong Metabolism Make Strong Ninja

Ideally, you would start building your Food Ninja before you even conceive a child. Hey, I'm not a good planner either, and my timing is always terrible. No really, I was a vegetarian when I worked in restaurants cooking foie gras and filet mignon, ate a low-carb diet when I lived in Hawaii and had tropical fruit trees in my yard, left Hawaii to try out some raw milk, and then ditched raw milk and now eat as much tropical fruit as I can. Bad timing I say. So it's okay if you're a little late to start Ninja training—meaning your kid has already been born. It's okay if you've also made a bunch of ridiculous eating mistakes with yourself and your kid. Odds are you probably had to before you even found a book like this. Most people check out that food pyramid thing, then some vegetarian books, then try low-carb, then try to be a caveman before they finally grab themselves a Matt Stone book and find it making the least bit of sense.

Well, it's not okay at all actually. That you were late to training. But hopefully me saying it's okay makes you feel better about your ignorance during the most pivotal times of Food Ninja development: before conception, during pregnancy, and during breastfeeding.

These are very important times because it is at these times that important metabolism programming takes place. Most of what we know about childhood obesity, type 2 diabetes, metabolic rate, and overall physical and mental prowess suggests that the vast majority of our health tendencies are forged long before we ever eat our first "junk food." Real researchers know this. I wouldn't even say it's debatable. Health gurus that believe in happily-ever-after fairy tales of eternal youth tend to deny this.

Well, of course our lifestyle and diet after the first year of life matters. There are lots of ways to make ourselves sicker or healthier depending on the routes we take. But some things are set in motion before you ever have any control over it personally, and thinking that you can just overcome some of your natural tendencies in adulthood is like thinking that there's a diet out there that is going to help you grow a 6th finger on each hand.

Okay, separate tangent for sure. Let's get back to your little Ninja.

As a prospective parent, a pregnant lady, or a breastfeeding mama—your focus needs to be on just a few simple things: a high metabolic rate and low levels of stress and inflammation. That's pretty much it. That and just making sure to take in lots of nutrients—but that will happen automatically if you are actively working on maximizing your metabolism.

Let's start with the most prominent of all food Ninja basics—the high metabolic rate.

High Metabolic Rate

There are a lot of misconceptions about metabolic rate, or metabolism. If you ask someone on the street what to do to raise metabolic rate, they will almost invariably say "exercise." If you ask people what foods to eat to raise metabolism, they will typically say "protein." Both of these are totally incorrect. Completely backwards. Both exercise and eating a lot of protein burn a lot of calories. Your metabolic rate is not how many calories you burn digesting protein or running around in circles out in the parking lot. That is your TEE, or total energy expenditure. Your metabolic rate is the amount of energy your body produces *at rest*. If resting metabolic rate was improved by eating lots of protein and exercising, athletes wouldn't have low resting pulse rates and low body temperatures (signs of reduced resting metabolic rate), but they typically do, particularly endurance athletes.

So yes, a high metabolic rate shouldn't be looked at as calories burned, but more like energy *produced*. Further refined, metabolic rate should be something that refers to cellular energy production, as the larger the creature, the more calories needed and thus the higher the resting metabolic rate if you are to go simply by total sum of energy required. But if it's not size-adjusted it is meaningless. In fact, the smaller the organism, usually the higher the cellular metabolic rate—the rate at which mitochondria produces energy.

This brings up yet another common misconception—the idea that building muscle increases metabolic rate because you are adding more tissue that needs to be fed. Adding muscle tissue doesn't mean that all the cells you had before are now producing more energy. In fact, they may be producing less energy to compensate for the extra muscle needing to be fed. You can't just get bigger to raise your resting metabolic rate in the true, size-adjusted sense.

Anywho, a high metabolic rate (rate of cellular energy turnover), from virtually all angles of investigation, is a powerful health asset. And metabolic rate is in severe decline, predominantly due to the diets and lifestyles of our parents it seems, and then exacerbated by the sadistic diet and exercise programs people typically follow when they start to get sick and chunky from their low metabolic rate.

Most people think of things we inherit from our parents as being "genetic." Yeah, my dad and I have the same size hands and feet and are exactly the same height. Neat. I clearly inherited some stuff from the dude. But what we inherit goes far beyond simple genetic material. There are influences with the quality of food we are fed as an infant (the quality of milk from mother to mother is radically different), and we inherit a lot of hormonal tendencies due to the influences of the intrauterine environment. For example, if mom restricts food intake while she's pregnant, that has an impact on the child. It lowers the child's metabolic rate, a perfectly smart adaptation to a world in which food is scarce. I'm telling you man. Our bodies know what this scarcity thing is, and they adapt to it quite well. Consider what was noted in the offspring of underfed pregnant women, from Ellen Ruppel Shell's *The Hungry Gene*:

"They made the rather startling discovery that adult children of mothers exposed to famine during the first two trimesters of their pregnancy were 80 percent more likely to be obese as adults… From this, the researchers theorized that

deprivation in the first two trimesters primed these famine victims for a life of scarcity. When food became plentiful after the war, this 'thrifty fetus' effect backfired, with obesity as the consequence. Later, scientists would also note higher rates of heart disease, diabetes, and other chronic disease and even mental illness..."

Simple enough, and makes perfect sense. We all know people who eat whatever they want and are very lean and energetic. As a parent to a Food Ninja, there is no greater gift that you can bestow upon your child than a high metabolic rate. As crappy as your metabolism may have been in your life, it is possible to hand off a much better metabolic rate to your offspring.

The formula for doing so is pretty straightforward and simple; send your body the *abundance* signal prior to and during pregnancy. The other primary factor involved is the composition of the fat in your body. The fat in human cells and tissues is a direct reflection of the type of fat we eat. Not all types of fat are created equal. The biological role of some fats, such as those found in nuts, seeds, and other things that germinate in cool soils (linoleic acid), is to lower metabolic activity. When animals that share similar physiology to humans eat lots of these foods at the end of the growing season each year, metabolic rate slows and they drift off into hibernation. Without this type of fat, their

metabolic rate will not slow down and they cannot hibernate successfully.
http://icb.oxfordjournals.org/content/38/2/331.full.pdf

Linoleic acid, until the early 20th century, was consumed by humans in fairly modest quantities. But consumption of the metabolically-suppressive linoleic acid has increased by a factor of ten or more since the widespread production of linoleic acid-rich oils from corn, soy, sunflower, cottonseed, canola, grapeseed, peanut, and others. This type of fat accumulates in tissues and has an adverse effect on metabolic rate. It is also worth noting that humans consume massive amounts of this type of fat 365 days per year, not seasonally like bears and squirrels fattening up for winter. The type of fat is totally ubiquitous to the modern food supply, found in mayonnaise, fried food, salad dressings, cookies, cakes, pastries, butter substitutes, crackers, chips, French fries, doughnuts, peanut butter, and

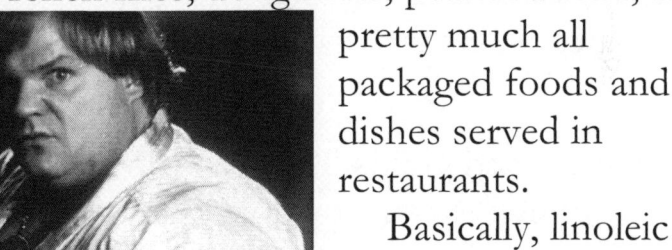

pretty much all packaged foods and dishes served in restaurants.

Basically, linoleic acid is a great substance for creating a Beverly Hills Ninja like Chris Farley. For a true Food

Ninja—strong, energetic, warm, lean, and sleek—it pays to spend some time purging your system of this fat before having kids, while pregnant, and while breastfeeding. All you have to do is eat considerably less of it. Very simple. The following 5 tips will give you the most bang for the least effort:

1. Stop buying and using oils that are liquid at room temperature (unless you buy macadamia nut oil or high oleic sunflower oil—a little olive oil is okay but don't overdo it), and cook your food at home in butter and coconut oil primarily.

2. Eat more food at home, and less at restaurants.

3. Decrease your intake of nuts, seeds, peanuts, and peanut butter. If you really like nuts and nut butters, macadamia nuts are the best option in that category by far.

4. Eat refined grains like white flour, white rice, and hominy instead of whole grain versions. Refining of grains removes the linoleic acid in grains. They also taste and digest better so this shouldn't take too much arm twisting to get you to try.

5. Reduce consumption of packaged foods. If you want to buy packaged foods, stick to packaged foods that are low in fat, like breakfast cereals, saltines, and pretzels instead of cookies, high-fat crackers, and chips.

By the way, the fatty foods that you do eat should come from mostly saturated sources: coconut, dairy fat including butter, cheese, etc., red meat from beef, bison, and lamb, and chocolate.

As far as raising metabolic rate by sending the abundance signal, that's even easier. Eat as much food as it takes to completely satisfy your appetite, eat often, and really emphasize sugar, starch, and salt in particular, with enough complementary protein and fat to make the food you eat taste great and feel complete.

Another important factor in metabolic rate is hydration. You hear tons about how we should all be chugging gallons of water day in and day out, but overhydrating to the point of making your urine clear lowers metabolic rate significantly, and can even cause dry skin (water is NOT a moisturizer!). By hydrating properly—not too much, not too little, with nice yellow urine each time, your metabolic rate will be significantly higher. Most can feel it immediately with warmer hands, feet, and body temperature—all prominent signs of operating from a more metabolically-active state.

And finally, no conversation on metabolic rate and abundance would be complete without talk of sleep and stress. Like I said, you don't raise your metabolic rate by running around in circles in a parking lot. If you want to raise your metabolic rate, you will need to keep exercise to moderate levels, making sure never to overdo it. You should spend more time doing things that are calming and relaxing. And speaking of calming and relaxing, there is no greater de-stressing, metabolism-stimulating tool than sleep. A surplus of sleep, along with a surplus of food, sends the abundance signal loud and clear, waking up even the most frozen and sluggish metabolisms.

You can monitor metabolic rate best by checking your body temperature and making sure it is at or around the normal 98.6F (37.0C). Higher temperatures are usually synonymous with even more impressive function. Maintaining a high metabolic rate will certainly send a very important abundance signal to your Ninja, a huge asset when he begins navigating his way through the modern food environment.

As a final note on metabolism for now, if all the lifestyle and dietary interventions fail, you might consider taking some thyroid medication. Cheating to get your metabolic rate up is still probably better than it remaining low.

Low Stress Levels

Yes, low stress levels are always going to be conducive to better health and vitality in a child. While forging your Ninja, sleep, sugar, starch, and salt (the Anti-Stress S's), relaxing activities, mental and emotional de-stressing work, and reasonable amounts of exercise are going to be the most effective tools that you have at your disposal. Calm mama make strong, emotionally-balanced Ninja.

Low Inflammation

There are opinions left and right about what causes inflammation, and how to reduce systemic inflammation. I've read so many theories and rants, and seen enough studies and articles on the topic that my head has been spun into a big cotton-candy-like blob of uncertainty. And that's probably a good thing. History shows us that the degree of certainty is usually correlated with the degree of error. Well, my history shows that at least.

When it comes to inflammation, I would again focus on the type of fatty acids you consume above other nutritional matters. Most inflammatory hormones in the body, such as the generally pro-inflammatory series of leukotreines, thromboxanes, prostaglandins, and other things with long names, are derived from a fatty acid known as Arachidonic Acid (AA). AA is ingested through food and is also constructed in the body from our buddy linoleic acid.

Eating very little linoleic acid helps. It also helps to eat less of the animals that are fed a bunch of linoleic acid, thus forming a lot of Arachidonic Acid in their fats: commercial poultry (the skin and organs in particular), commercial eggs, commercial pork, organ meats, and farmed fish. But note, even "happy pigs" and "happy chickens" can still be fed a lot of corn and soy and have the same fatty acid profiles in their cells and tissues as the stuff coming out of big factories. You don't have to avoid these foods religiously, or neurotically, but don't overdo it. There are certainly a lot of health nerds out there consuming their bodyweight each year in duck fat, lard, chicken skin, bacon, organ meats, and eggs. Beef, cheese, and seafood for me in that department, especially as someone who grew up with lots of allergies, asthma, and physical pain. A diet high in AA is supposedly enough to increase the inflammatory response to a potential trigger.

"Research has proven that a high AA diet has the potential actually to change normal immune responses to abnormal, exaggerated ones. A study carried out in 1997 by Dr. Darshan S. Kelley and colleagues at the Western Human Nutrition Research Center in California showed that people on high-AA diets generated four times as many

inflammatory cells after a flu vaccination as people on low-AA diets."
      ~Floyd Chilton; *Inflammation Nation*

 Regardless of what nutritional philosophy you are currently guided by, the most important thing, as an expecting parent (mom or dad), and as a pregnant mom, is that you *don't diet!* By diet I mean restrict calorie intake primarily. And don't get too strict with avoiding certain macronutrients either. Yeah, the Inuit ate hardly any carbohydrates at all, and rural Africans, in all their glistening white-toothed glory, ate hardly any fat. That doesn't mean that you can get away with strict restrictions. You'll probably find that the more extreme you get, the lower that body temperature drops.
 And forget about eating perfectly "clean." Even a seemingly-healthy diet full of salads and vegetables and low-sugar berries overflowing with antioxidants can lead to accidental undereating by virtue of the fact that those foods are appetite deterrents. I know you want to eat the most pure and wholesome diet that you can, but this is about priorities and picking the right battles, and nothing is more primary than calorie intake. To prepare a kid for Ninja warfare in the modern food environment, you're truly better off focusing on metabolic rate above all other factors. Eat food that

you love and crave—those calorie-dense gems that pack a big energy punch.

This is a pretty good summary of what you can do to pre-Ninjify your child. But, as you'll see in the next chapter, many of these same principles apply to a mother's diet, lifestyle, and metabolism during the first year of lil' Ninja life.

Level 2: Ninja Need Special Ninja Milk

If you want a Food Ninja, you can't be nursing her with watered down vegetable oil breast "product" disguised as mother's milk. And you most certainly can't feed the young warrior-to-be formula, which is a formula for failure.

Over the past century an alarming trend has taken place with human breast milk. It continues to contain greater and greater quantities of linoleic acid. Here is a graph showing the changing fatty acid composition of breast milk over the last several decades:

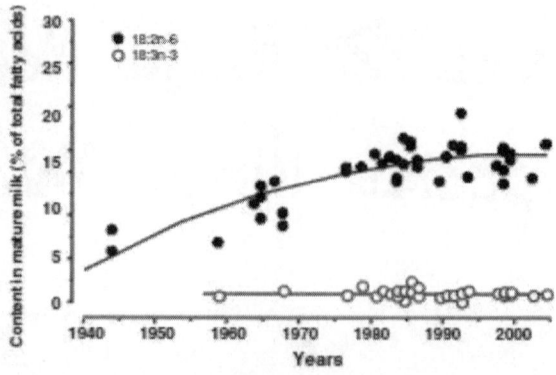

You can see that in 1940, the total percentage of fatty acids as linoleic acid (the black dots) was slightly above 5%, and has later moved up to 15% of fatty acids or higher. Unfortunately, infant formula has changed over the years as well to approximate this progressively-crappier milk. Manufacturers of formula are now talking about ramping up the corn oil in formula to 20%. That'll be a winning move for sure, if you call getting a roundhouse to the temple and a face full of nunchuck fury "winning." I call it defeat.

What's particularly awesome about linoleic acid is that the content of linoleic acid in milk predicts the size and number of fat cells in the infant— probably the best indicator of one's obesity proneness later in life. And it's true that future body fatness can be predicted very well in young children by early surveys of body composition, even before they eat their first Happy Meal or suck down their first Coca-Cola (the usual suspects). This all comes right back to our conversation about changing the fatty acid composition in your tissues the best you can.

If you get 2% of your dietary calories from linoleic acid, you'll probably have milk closer to 2% linoleic acid. The higher your LA consumption (please don't make me write linoleic again), the higher that percentage will go. While you can't totally avoid LA in the real world unless you cast yourself into health fanatic exile, at the very least you can improve your breast milk, and an improvement, even a slight improvement, is enough to give the Ninja-to-be a fighting chance.

Changes in the fatty acid composition of your cells and tissues don't happen overnight. Some of the most studious of academics on this subject still believe that it can take, not months, but *years* to purify your body of this stuff. So be patient and be realistic. Focus on the simple and doable five changes outlined earlier, and you will make some headway.

Another thing I wanted to mention again was the overhydration thing. Nursing moms are often told to chug massive amounts of water against their will to "keep milk supply up." While I'm certain that dehydration is terrible, and wouldn't want to make anyone afraid of drinking water while nursing, I've gotta think that quality is being overlooked in pursuit of quantity. Milk is not just milk. In fact, you can feel this for yourself by playing around with the calorie-density of milk. The more calories there are in a glass of milk, the more metabolically-stimulating it is. Get a thermometer out and see. The more calories you squeeze into an 8-ounce glass the hotter you get, generally-speaking. You want concentrated diesel, bulletproof breast milk, not watered down, empty fluid—unless you want a cold, lifeless monk for a child.

I won't drone on and on in this chapter, as basically the same factors influencing metabolism, stress, and inflammation in the mother influence the very same things in the quality of the mother's breast milk and the metabolism of the child. Eat big, sleep hard, clean out the linoleic acid, and take it easy. Perhaps surprisingly if you are of the "must starve thyself to lose weight" paradigm, doing this will usually lead to greater postpartum fat loss while nursing.

One last question we must address here though, is what to do if you are unable to nurse, or find that your breast milk quality, try as you might, sucks. While it may seem sacrilege to recommend the milk of another mammal in lieu of a specially-failure-formulated concoction sold at your local Wal-Mart, I can't imagine, armed with this knowledge, that you couldn't create a better formula on your own.

Primates that we are, our milk differs from other mammals primarily by being exceptionally sweet. In fact, the composition of human breast milk is almost identical to that of typical ice cream in every way, including vitamin and mineral levels and proportions. Put a more specific way, the ratio of sugar (lactose) to protein in milk is very high. In humans it is somewhere between 6-7:1 carbohydrate to protein, whereas in goat milk, standard references show a ratio of about 1.25:1 carb to protein. Cow's milk is roughly 1.5:1, still not nearly as sweet as human milk.

While nursing conveys benefits to the infant that don't show up on paper, such as mother-child bonding, antibody and live beneficial bacteria, and so forth, many kids should thrive on something like fresh, unpasteurized goat milk with enough powdered lactose added to make the carbohydrate to protein ratio fall in the 6-7:1 range. It should taste sweet, like ice cream, and will have all the vitamins and minerals a growing kid could need—plus a glorious 1.4% linoleic acid content. That's what I'm talkin' bout. I'd much rather give that to a young Ninja than the milk of some mom whose fingers are stained orange from Cheeto dust.

Okay, I'll stop before the head of the La Leche League reads this and either spontaneously combusts or dispatches a mob of angry women to my house. Wait a sec, those women would probably be lactating. Come on over ladies! Leave your walnuts (50% LA, often touted as "a good source of omega 3's") and fish oil at the door. A keg of coconut oil awaits!

Okay, that was weird. But seriously, I'm almost 36 and have never tried breast milk. Not a single drop in my life. It just feels like something's missing. I will continue to have an outspoken fetish with lactating women until I've tried it. Don't judge me man. You don't know what it's like!

Level 3: Ninja Is Not Mr. Sailor Man

Seriously moms and dads, you have to stop trying to force feed or bribe your kids to eat vegetables. *"Okay, lil' Johnny, two more big bites of broccoli and you can have some ice cream!"*

For starters, why are vegetables so awesome? Because eating bland stuff makes you healthier? I'm not saying they are inherently unhealthy or anything, but you have got to trust the instincts of children. Their bodies are much smarter than your minds. Don't you remember back when you hated a bunch of foods as a kid, and then, as you got older, your tastes changed to accommodate a much greater diversity of foods? Kids don't have the kind of digestive prowess that adults do, and their taste buds are a lot more sensitive. They don't necessarily want to be choking down a bunch of indigestible cellulose filled with bitter compounds like oxalic acid (found in large amounts in spinach, the staple of that cartoon character with disproportional forearms).

And even if they did, the typical knuckle-dragging parenting tactic of bribing kids to eat veggies will pretty much kill any chance they could have had for enjoying them. Turning something into work, or a means to an end—"Finish your veggies and then you can watch TV!" decreases the pleasure one derives from it. Offering up a reward makes whatever is used as a reward more attractive, and whatever you need to do to obtain it less attractive. If you want your kids to be TV and ice cream junkies, keep offering them up as rewards. Or tell them yummy foods are bad for them and that they are not allowed to eat them. Set 'em up for a good, hearty binge. All of these well-intentioned interventions have the exact opposite impact as intended.

The seminal work on this kind of thing is Alfie Kohn's *Punished by Rewards*, a book that should be required reading for any parent, with the same rules applying to behavior and education as applies to eating (Want a kid to hate reading? Give them a reward for doing it or punish them by making them do it. Works every time!).

All that aside, we can sidestep any parenting and human psychology and behavior debates and continue to put vegetables in their rightful nutritional place. Vegetables are low-grade food barely worth eating. They are empty filler that pack very little in terms of real, usable energy.

Oh wait. I can hear it coming already.

"Empty? Empty! Vegetables are full of very important vitamins and minerals!"

Yeah yeah. The same person who will fight tooth and nail in advocacy of breastfeeding a child until they are practically in college also tends to believe that a kid's solid food diet must be comprised of all these incredibly nutrient-dense foods, boasting about how junior "doesn't care for ice cream and loves steamed broccoli and spinach."

Broccoli smoccoli. Spinach winnich. You watched too many episodes of Popeye. You don't see Chuck Norris talking about his secret weapon being spinach. Even if he did eat it, he wouldn't talk about it. Chuck lets his fists do the talking. He did once patent a martial arts move designed to scratch hard-to-reach bug bites. He calls it the Spin Itch.

Okay, back off. I'm really trying here. It's a ninja book. Clearly Chuck Norris was going to make an appearance.

All the nutrients a growing kid needs are found in breast milk, which has, like I pointed out earlier, the same nutrient density as a bowl of ice cream! Ice cream! Ice cream with 40% of its calories coming from zero-nutrient white sugar! And that's to grow fresh bones, teeth, and tissue. Maintaining is even easier! People are obsessed with these vitamins and minerals like there is some kind of health and longevity award awaiting the person who manages to consume the most in a single lifetime. Oh stop it. Just eat. You'll get plenty of nutrients as long as you aren't subsisting on snack cakes and Mountain Dew exclusively. And so will your Ninja. Food Ninjas don't need extra nutrients. They need extra calories.

Ice cream to the rescue!

 A couple of years ago I did a Skype video call with a big, health-conscious family. Mom was clearly fanatical about health. I could see that right away. And there, alongside of her was her son. Kid could have worn a Cheerio for a necklace. He was pale, skin and bones, and looked lifeless and anemic. Then she started talking about the kind of foods they eat at home.
 "Well, we eat lots of quinoa, he loves avocado…"
 I wanted to stab my ears with butter knives. I cut her off quickly. The problem was obvious and was very serious. This kid had almost bled to death recently from extremely low platelets that mystified his doctors.

I inquired more about his true favorites. Mom mentioned ice cream among other kid classics, but mentioned not really letting him have those types of things very often. My suggestion was to keep all of his favorite foods around and try to provide the most enjoyable eating experience as possible. Within a week, he improved dramatically, lifting his platelets from rock bottom up nearly into the normal range. The food he ate the most of, by far, was ice cream.

But a month or so later, something interesting happened. He started to regress somewhat, for reasons we will delve into deeper later when we discuss palatability. In short, he got sick of ice cream. The family had been looking at it as a medicinal food of sorts and kept feeding and feeding and feeding it to him. Guess what? He got sick of it. Ice cream was only medicinal because it made him eat more. But that's where the magic ended. Soon they were giving him a variety of foods that he wanted, when he was in the mood for them. He stopped downsliding and went on to do great, overcoming his low platelet condition completely according to my last communication with the family.

Moral of the story: calories are primary in the health of your child. Calories, and the macronutrients: protein, fat, and carbohydrates, are the primary nutrients we derive from food. Micronutrients: vitamins and minerals, are secondary and typically obtained in sufficient amounts just from eating a diverse range of foods. Don't get too caught up on feeding your kid what the mainstream, starvation-fetish-havin' nutrition authorities believe. Their food needs to be good and calorie-dense for them to live up to their maximum potential.

Vegetables aside, what are some good feeding guidelines to go by when it comes to feeding a future Kung-Food master? Without dissecting it to the point of obscene and unnecessary detail, here are what I consider to be the four primary basics worthy of your focus: adaptability, palatability, neutrality, and performance.

Adaptability

One skill that you and your Food Ninja must develop is that of adaptability. If a person eats an all-vegetable diet, they will adapt to that diet somewhat. If a person eats an all-meat diet, a person adapts to that somewhat. If someone is on a raw food diet, they will get sick if they eat cooked food. You get the idea. But a true modern Food

Ninja must be adapted to the modern food environment, and be able to handle just about anything with a wide range of metabolic and digestive flexibility. Or, in the words of Dr. Henry Bieler when describing someone of excellent metabolic health and adaptability: *"He may and often does boast that he can eat any and all kinds of food without discomfort... He can dine on the most impossible food combinations imaginable with no evil results."*

Do you really want to raise a kid that feels ill if they eat out at a restaurant, at a friend's house, or eat anything other than their specially-formulated homemade "health food?" On the opposite end of the spectrum, would you want a kid to get a stomachache from eating a lettuce leaf because they are used to only eating processed food? Of course not. You want your kid to be healthy, attractive, and as carefree and spontaneous as possible. I believe that many people can have it all, and the number of people that are just "so lucky" that they can eat whatever they want without becoming fat or ill doesn't have to be so small. In fact, the majority of us could do exactly that—eat what we want, when we want, and have nothing but health and energy to show for it with the right tactics in childhood and adulthood.

What this boils down to when it comes to putting something into real-world practice with your kid is making sure that his or her food environment is diverse and exciting. It should contain plenty of the quintessential wholesome foods. It should have stuff that's hard to chew and digest. It should contain stuff so processed you hardly have to chew it at all. It should contain super calorie-dense food bombs like that served at every kid's party. It should contain massive loads of rapidly-absorbed carbohydrates. It should contain low glycemic carbohydrates. The kid should be able to eat all day or not eat all day and still be fairly solid and resilient. Etc. Etc. Etc.

The end result is that the kid should have the digestive and metabolic machinery to pretty much annihilate anything. Just like Sho Nuff at his best in the movie *The Last Dragon* when his metabolism gets so high his fingertips start to glow like molten

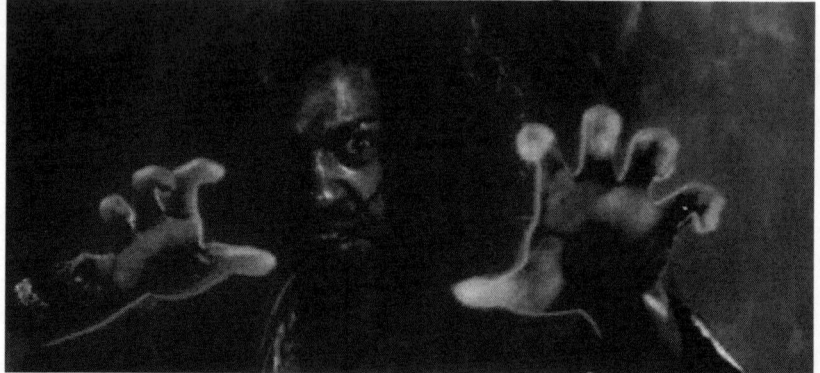

metal. Note, this took place shortly after he and his gang pillaged a pizza place. Coincidence? Without a doubt. And has nothing to do with anything. But I watched the movie excessively as a kid so you are just going to have to sit through pointless tangents about it.

Oh, you think because it's a new paragraph I'm done with the tangent? Okay, yes I am done with the tangent. You're right. I hate it when you're right.

So give the kid a wide variety of things. All kinds of different tastes and textures all varying in calorie-density. Of course, you want most of the food in your own home to be prepared with minimal amounts of linoleic acid. That much we can control without driving ourselves, wait for it, NUTS. And you want it to be predominantly nutritious food. But you don't want to get too overly puritanical or the kid will get too inflexible and bored. You want to get lots of store-bought ice cream and candy from time to time. You want to order pizza. You want to go out for burgers and fries. And no modern childhood is complete without some glowing orange cheese dust from time to time.

Palatability

We already touched on this a little, but this is something to keep in the forefront of your mind. This is of even greater importance in a young kid who is plagued with poor digestion and obvious signs of a low metabolism, typical in kids who are underweight. Above almost every other concern, the food must taste good!

There's no question as far as I'm concerned that the world's most elite physical specimens, and the world's elite lean, mean, eating machines, need a solid abundance of calories. Calories are the base material for which all energy is produced in the body. Can you really picture a professional athlete ordering a chicken Caesar salad? It just doesn't happen. The formula for ultimate vitality is, quite simply, to play hard, eat hard, and sleep hard. And that all begins with food that tastes good, because you can't play hard without eating hard, and you can't sleep hard without eating hard (and playing hard).

While the calorie-phobic, obesity-paranoid parent may be mired in the belief that eating too much leads to fatness and health problems (that are way too hastily pinned on obesity), at least consider the fact that kids' diets have become considerably lower in calories and carbohydrates in particular from 1999-2010 in the U.S., in all age groups of kids, all with a corresponding rise in obesity, type 2 diabetes, asthma, and more.

http://www.cdc.gov/nchs/data/databriefs/db113.htm

Then take a deep breath and get ready to watch your kids thrive eating more, becoming metabolic dynamos, running around with energy and upbeat dispositions, and using the food they ingest for energy, heat, strong bones and teeth, and toned muscles. Any leftover gets passed out in stool or causes a slight drop in appetite. That's how an organism is built to work. All you have to do is trust it. Shouldn't be hard when your infant comes programmed to suck on things to obtain milk. No graduate degree or certification required to figure out what and how to eat. Your Ninja kid is smart. Bow down.

So yes, just as has always been believed, a "healthy appetite" is a sign of health. Your kids will invariably thrive on a higher-calorie diet more than they will on a lower-calorie diet. And the primary controller of how many calories a child will eat is how palatable the food is.

Taste, temperature, texture, smell—lots of things determine the palatability of any given food. But ultimately palatability is a moving target, and is different for every individual every day. Scientifically, ice cream fits the description of a palatable food. Creamy, delicious, sweet, super calorie-dense. But not everyone likes it. I love it! For a few days. Then I can hardly look at it for a month. Seriously. And I once avoided it for years because I thought I was "addicted" to it. Ha!

To be an ultimate Ninja feeder, it's important that you are giving the kid stuff she wants, likes, and happens to be in the mood for. With a big family, you can't be a short-order cook making what every single person wants. You won't see me making two different dishes for dinner, much less a different food for every person in a family of ten. But at least hook the kid up sometimes, especially if she has been a little bored with her food for a while.

A key element to stress with feeding a kid is *variety*. If you put one simple food in front of anyone, they will get full and bored with the meal long before they reach a high calorie level. Think of scrambled eggs. If someone put a plate of scrambled eggs in front of you and that's all you were allowed to eat, how many calories would you consume before you quit and moved onto a more interesting activity? But if you add a chocolate chip pancake, a glass of orange juice—now we're talkin'! You might eat twice as much total food, maybe more. So make sure that meals have more than just one component. Make them as "square" as you can, within reason.

Along the same lines is making sure that each food has multiple elements. Take the pancakes I mentioned above. Dry on a plate? Eck. But covered with fresh fruit, warm maple syrup, and salted butter? The kid will karate chop that pancake with no mercy. No mercy! Mercy is for the weak.

Come on, you had to have seen that line coming. I'm trying my best here to let you know these punches are coming so you can block them. I'm not like Chong Li, throwing some blinding powder in your eyes. I'm giving you a sporting chance to defend yourselves here.

Anyway, make it yummy. That's all I'm saying. Surely you know what is and isn't yummy and will be able to relay some of that to the kid. Then watch and observe what the kid's favorites are and be there to provide them to the best of your ability.

If all else fails, just put a good blend of starch, sugar, salt, and saturated fat on the table. Should disappear pretty quickly.

Neutrality

This strikes really near and dear to my heart. Like a Ninja dagger. Most parents have an idea about what is and is not healthy.

"Sugar is a toxin! Pasteurized milk is inferior! You gotta eat your vegetables! Here, have an apple for dessert!"

Or they think it's good to eat a lot, or not good to eat a lot.

"You are gonna sit at that table until you finish your dinner young man! No Ralph, only a kiddie cup. No waffle cones! You're gonna get fat!"

Sometimes these ideas change like the wind. Or they never change, which is even worse because the same foods are restricted throughout a kid's entire childhood. Some parents will tell their kids to stop eating so much food, and then get them all excited to go out for ice cream with a tone of voice that sounds like someone has just won the lottery. It's all a big mess.

Stop it. All food should be on an even playing field. There are no good and bad foods. By chastising bad foods, you create complex emotional/psychological chain reactions that result in impaired eating behavior. One of the greatest downsides to being highly intelligent, self-aware creatures is our ability to interfere with instincts that are perfectly capable of performing a job correctly. Just step aside. The act of eating should be as emotionally and psychologically neutral as possible, especially for a young child that is still untainted by thought for food.

Food is also NOT entertainment. It's not "bad," but it's not a source of pornographic pleasure either. Just let it be neutral. If it's not, you run the risk of interfering with appetite and satiety cues and disrupting the whole energy-balancing system with a multi-million year track record of success.

Certainly don't interfere with food quantity on any conscious level. If a kid wants to eat, let her eat. If she doesn't, don't force her.

Seriously though, create a neutral eating environment for your kids with the absolute minimum amount of psychological interference. They will not eat a steady diet of jelly beans if you fail to mention how horrible refined sugar is. My girlfriend's kid wouldn't be any less excited about Halloween if people handed out wheat grass shots to trick-or-treaters. 'Cause whatever she gets, she doesn't touch. The kids that have spent a year on the GAPS diet or some other barbaric regimen are the ones with the blue raspberry Nerd-stained tongues at the end of the night, accompanied by headaches, bellyaches, and a sore throat the next morning.

Performance

It's neato to talk about all this stuff in a general sense, but ultimately, what matters most above all else is the end result. The kid needs to have an exceptionally high metabolic rate and be healthy and vibrant with as few problems as possible. Here are some of the best indicators of metabolic health that you can be attentive to for signs of success—what I call the Metabolism Report Card (Kid Version):

1. Oral/rectal/ear/forehead temperature should be at least 98.6 degrees F/37.0 C at all times.

2. Hands and feet should typically feel warm at normal room temperature. Skin in other parts of the body should feel warm to the touch as well, like a little living radiator.

3. Hair and fingernails should be fast-growing, with good shine to the hair and hardness to the nails.

4. The kid should have multiple bowel movements every day that are quick, easy, large, and soft with no odor and very little wiping required. Stomach bloating after meals, excessive gas production, and any sign of stomach pain should be minimal or nonexistent.

5. Your Ninja should urinate roughly once every four hours during the day, never at night (bedwetting), with no strong urges. The color should be yellow, never pale or clear.

6. Your child should be able to sleep through the night—a solid 10+ hours (or more depending on age) with no wakeups, nightmares, or night terrors.

7. Mood should be very stable and upbeat except in very stressful situations—like after a night of staying up too late or going far too long without food. Energy levels should also follow this pattern.

8. The kid should have a thicker build—not fat nor gangly and emaciated-looking, with decent muscularity and a relatively flat stomach.

9. The kid should rarely, if ever, get sick from any of the typical colds, flus, ear and sinus infections, and so forth. The kid should obviously not suffer from a cluster of chronic conditions either, like asthma, allergies, eczema, and others.

10. The kid should eat what seems like an impossible amount of fattening food without gaining a single ounce of body fat. If you ever track calorie consumption out of curiosity, you should see intakes upwards of 30 calories per pound of bodyweight per day depending on activity levels and age (the younger they are, the more they eat per pound of bodyweight).

There are dozens more of course, but these are pretty primary and easy to monitor for signs of improvement with any kind of strategies that you implement for your kids.

Food Ninja or not, we've all got to do the best with what we've got. While becoming a successful Food Ninja is the ultimate goal, it's unreasonable to think that every person can succeed in getting there. Some just don't have the makeup to be a successful Food Ninja to the fullest.

There are a lot of messed up kids these days, and you shouldn't expect that taking your really ill autistic 6-year old son off of the FODMAPS diet or whatever that thing is called will solve all his problems. I don't expect, at 35 years of age, to have my horrendous eyesight correct itself by eating my bodyweight in blueberries.

I'm getting at just a couple simple points here. One is that there is no single cure-all solution, and you should be realistic.

Secondly, you, as a parent, have veto power over everything you encounter. I wouldn't want you blindly following this "prescription" so-to-speak with no regard for how the kid is responding. You are the ultimate expert. You can see and observe junior's changes in diet satisfaction, craving intensity, binge-proneness, sleep quality, behavior, susceptibility to colds and flu, body temperature, and other key markers of health and a good relationship with food. You're there to observe from minute to minute, hour to hour, day to day, week to week, and beyond. No one knows your child better than you, and no outside authority that has never even met your child and has no knowledge of any specific details can do a better job than you. Nor can your doctor in most cases, as a 30-minute office visit and a few tests (often just meaningless snapshots) can only relay so much information to someone who has no clue about the subtle nuances of your child's well-being.

Level 4: Ninja Is Not Fish

This is not a huge issue. I won't dwell on it. Odds are if you take even the slightest little bit of the information in this book to heart, you will also have some respect for Ninja junior's ability to regulate his or her own hydration levels. If mice can do it successfully, I'm pretty sure we humans can, too.

I've written extensively about the dangers of overhydration in other materials of mine. Overhydration in young children is actually quite common, and one of the most frequent causes of seizures in infants. Even small amounts of water will cause an infant to seize the day, because it dilutes body fluids and creates a state in the body known as hyponatremia—when that salty water inside of us gets flooded and dangerously diluted. In the brain it causes swelling, and that's when the headaches and migraines and seizures and strange behavior commence.

When my girlfriend's daughter was still going to public school, the weather got extremely hot towards the end of the school year. The teachers took it upon themselves to force all the children to drink copious amounts of water to prevent dehydration and heat exhaustion while playing on the playground. Everyone knows the dangers of these villains, but nobody EVER hears anything about the danger of recklessly overhydrating unfortunately. Emily wasn't used to drinking water for starters. It wasn't something her body was very well-adapted to. As a less than 50-pound kid, she didn't drink fluids in very large amounts at all.

Lots and lots and lots of water in her, we went to school to pick her up. We walked across town to a restaurant and sat down for dinner. She repeatedly got up to go to the bathroom and complained of being very cold (even though it wasn't cold at all). She was acting very weird and distant and mentioned having a headache. After dinner she took off down the street toward home without giving much of a warning. We found her school backpack and something she was carrying by hand along the way on the ground. These were occurrences we have never seen before or since.

She continued to act very strange and insisted on having several blankets over her (the thermostat was set to 78 degrees F). That night she was up all night peeing, 4-5 times at least. It was real fun for everyone involved.

But we didn't understand what was going on in the slightest. We were really worried. It wasn't until later that we found out the school was forcing her to drink copious amounts of water at recess. This may sound dramatic and extreme, but it's not really. People all over the world are inducing chronic issues with headaches, migraines, dizzy spells, insomnia (from having to pee all night long), and other quite serious problems simply from forcing down a quantity of fluid that they believe to be mandatory for good health. There is no finer example of intellect interfering with instinct for dismal results than the fluid issue. What's particularly scary about it all is that entering a very overhydrated state can lead to an extremely dry mouth—not unlike how licking your lips repeatedly can lead to dry lips, or showering too much can cause dry skin.

So please, don't ever force your kid to drink. The only time a little extra fluid can be helpful is when you know that you are about to go out in the heat, or you can confirm that they are dehydrated (haven't peed in hours, dark urine, etc.). But even in that circumstance, the quantity of fluids your kid should drink should be small. The younger the kid, the more important this becomes, as the smaller the buffer system, the more problematic excess fluid consumption becomes.

In some cases it might be prudent to *feed* kids when they get excessively thirsty. If they consume too many fluids, or too little food, that dry mouth will hit them and they might want to drink themselves silly despite peeing clear every 15 minutes. Keep an eye on this. If a child's hands and feet are very cold, they are urinating frequently or have problems with bedwetting, you are better to give them a concentrated snack when they are complaining of thirst, or at least a snack with their drink. The snack should be very dry and feature lots of rapidly-absorbed carbohydrates and salt. Saltines and cheese, pretzels and candy—these have a much better chance at returning the child to normalcy quickly. Again, don't get too caught up on food quality here or anything like that. In an emergency situation where the body is in a very stressed state (urinating frequently is a good sign of being in this state), the more refined and rapidly-absorbed the food is, the faster it gets into the bloodstream and turns down the outpouring of adrenal hormones.

In very extreme circumstances, such as an unprovoked temper tantrum or other emotional outburst seemingly without cause, or when your kid is acting extremely weird and stressed and won't eat, you may have to resort to Ninja tactics. A little 10:1 mixture of white sugar and salt (Morton's

Canning and Pickling Salt has the most pleasant taste of the cheap salts) thrown into the mouth works great. It may seem a little harsh, but it's a good lesson for parents. Many of you who grab your child and shove a spoonful of this mixture in their mouths will quickly learn that the child's behavior has nothing to do with them being rotten little buttholes, and everything to do with them being in a compromised physical state. When a child is truly "crashing," Ninja Powder hitting the tongue is like Daniel Larusso hitting slabs of ice. Usually hits them within 30 seconds and they start behaving in a calm and serene way. The younger the kid, the more apparent the effects of this tactic are.

Also try to trust what kids prefer to drink. When a person is in poor metabolic condition, they usually crave and need very sweet drinks. Fruit juice, Gatorade, even soft drinks are a better option than plain water for some people, as ridiculous as that may sound to you. Ask your Ninja what he wants. Sometimes it will be milk, sometimes chocolate milk, sometimes Coke, sometimes fruit juice, and, believe it or not, sometimes regular old plain and boring water. When a kid doesn't know that one type of drink is "bad" and another is "good" you'll see a variety of selections. Milkshakes count as beverages as well. Some kids need and thrive off of that kind of calorie density. At least until they become metabolic black belts.

Okay, I said I wasn't going to dwell on this topic. I'm starting to run the risk of breaking this promise. As a final word, what matters the most is the end result. The kid should be urinating once every four hours during the day, none at night (certainly no bedwetting), and it should have some nice yellow color to it each time. As a parent, that is your goal with hydrating your kid. You're most likely to hit that target by getting out of the way and letting the kid's instincts take over. But there are circumstances where you might need to intervene ever-so-slightly to assist your child in returning to the optimal state of hydration—not too much, not too little.

But one thing is for certain. Your kid is not a fish. Don't drown your Ninja. That is a much more frequent mistake being committed by health conscious "good parents" trying to be proactive.

Level 5: Ninja Training

Your Food Ninja has been built. Now it's time for training. Digestive training, metabolic training, and physical training. Putting it all together now for full Ninja competency.

I know in some sense, in the back of your mind, all this sounds a little bit ridiculous. But I want you to really think about why the things that are stated in this book are stated in this book. Really think about the strategy here, and the lifestyle afforded to your child, if he or she truly becomes one of the lucky ones that eats everything in sight and still manages to have visible abs year round, during both times of great physical activity and physical inactivity. There are really people like that. They are few. I believe this book holds the keys to increasing that number and paving the way for our world's future. It should be taken seriously. You may disagree, but keep in mind that I know a lot more than you do (I don't mean you Ray, if you're reading this. I mean everyone else), so you should be pretty timid and tentative in your disagreements.

I want you, as a parent, and as a person, to strive for the greatest possible outcome before giving up and making compromises. Sure, maybe your kid can't eat "X" food without vomiting, no matter how much Food Ninja training she has undertaken. I get that. Some people will have to be on special diets and endure the unpleasantness of it for their best health outcome. Not everyone can have it all, but some can, especially those that get off to a good start with well-fed, hypermetabolic parents and rocket fuel breast milk.

With that said, here are four tests that your kid must pass before they can become certified Food Ninjas:

1) The Cookie Test

A child can pass the cookie test by declining a cookie when offered, giving it to you or a sibling untouched, or eating part of the cookie but not finishing it. A Food Ninja should like cookies and be able to eat enormous quantities of them in certain circumstances. But it should just be an edible disc, and one that is not at all interesting when there is no appetite. A Food Ninja eats because they are hungry and in the mood. They will not just eat a cookie because it is in front of them. If there is a cookie jar it should be out in the open and in plain view and easy to reach. You shouldn't have to worry about cookies disappearing at a fast rate in your household if everyone is Ninja Certified.

If your child currently eats cookies like Cookie Monster and you are terrified that he will eat his way to 1,000 pounds if left to eat as many as he desires, it's time to face your fear. Make cookies his shadow until he is bored with them and passes the test. It should only take a week if done thoroughly, with cookies always available. I refer to this as the feedbag method, inspired in part by the real-world truth that I've witnessed countless times in the M&M pillowcase story from Geneen Roth's *When Food is Love*:

"My friend Clara told me a story about a client of hers, an eight-year-old child who had been on a diet for two years and had gained fourteen pounds in the process. In desperation, her mother consulted Clara; Clara asked what her daughter's favorite food was. 'M&Ms,' the mother replied.

'Good, I want you to leave here and buy enough M&Ms to fill a pillowcase. After you've done that, give the filled pillowcase to your daughter and let her eat the candy whenever she wants. As soon as the supply is diminished, refill it. Make sure she always has a full pillowcase of M&Ms. Take her off the diet, let her eat whatever she wants when she is hungry, and call me in a week.'

After shrieking with horror and telling Clara that if her daughter gained fifty pounds, she was going to send her to live at Clara's house, the mother crept out of Clara's office, into a supermarket, and then home to her linen closet.

Her daughter carried the pillowcase of M&Ms around with her for eight days. She slept with it, she set it beside the tub when she took a bath, she put it in a chair when she watched television. And, of course, she helped herself to M&Ms whenever she wanted them. Which, the first few days, was very often. In fact, after her mother bought three more pounds of M&Ms on the third day of this sugar-coated experience, she was ready to sue Clara. In a hysterical phone call, she told her that her child was eating more candy than ever before and how the hell was she supposed to lose weight doing this? Clara reassured her that her daughter was reacting to the years of deprivation and that when she believed, really believed, that she could eat whatever she wanted and that her mother was not waiting to snatch her pillowcase away, she would relax and begin eating from stomach hunger.

On the ninth day, the pillowcase stayed in the bedroom. By the end of five weeks, her daughter had forgotten the M&Ms and had lost six pounds."

2) The Halloween Candy Test

Similar to the cookie test, a Food Ninja can take or leave a bucket of candy. There should be candy left in the bucket from Halloween the year before. If you get ready for Halloween and there is candy in the trick or treat bag from the prior year, and the kid had easy access to eat it all year long as desired, your Food Ninja has passed the Halloween candy test.

3) The McDonald's Test

McDonald's is an incredibly enticing dining experience for a young kid. Toys? A playground? Super calorie-dense food seasoned to absolute perfection with flavor enhancers and processed to the point of hardly needing teeth to chew? It's hard to compete with Ronald. You can try to completely avoid the place if you want, but wouldn't it be more empowering to know that your child is already bored to tears with the place before she reaches adulthood? In 2012 I got tired of hearing the "I want to go to McDonald's" chants coming from the booster seat behind me. Hell, this kid was talking about McDonald's like a long lost love. Something had to be done. And something was done. We ate every, and I mean EVERY meal at McDonald's until she practically begged us to stop going. When we went, we stayed there as long as she wanted. One day we spent four or five hours at McDonald's while she played in the stupid plastic tubes. Brutal, but probably saved me 100 hours of having to go there over the next decade.

Through it all, which included two McNugget ejections by the 4th consecutive day (mom and I didn't feel so hot either to be honest, but at least kept our drawers white) we found that she didn't even really care much for the food. She was there for the toys and playground. A year later she is pretty indifferent about the place, and, even though she just turned 8, she no longer even bothers to get a Happy Meal. Just a cheeseburger and the occasional milkshake—the two lowest sources of vegetable oil in the whole joint.

For your child to pass the McDonald's test, you must say "Would you like to go to McDonald's?" and the answer from the booster seat in the back must be "no." Doesn't have to happen every time, but that first "no" is a sign that McBalance has been achieved.

4) The Calorie Test

Your kid has shown great neutrality with food if she has passed the first three tests. But the psychological aspects of eating are only part of being a true Food Ninja. To become a food Ninja, you have to be able to display great courage in the face of tremendous calories. In order to pass the calorie test, your child must consume at least 20 calories per pound of bodyweight in a single sitting without digestive upset or any signs of fatigue or malaise. And your child, if under the age of 10, should also be observed eating between 30-40 calories per pound of bodyweight per day on a regular basis. Maybe more. All of this is done, mind you, with zero fat gain.

5) The Skipped Meal Test

A Food Ninja does best eating frequently and having regular meals, breakfast in particular. The old adage that breakfast is the most important meal of the day still rings true and is backed up by more and more evidence. Despite all this, a true Food Ninja has the metabolic flexibility to cope with change. To pass the skipped meal test, your Food Ninja must miss a regular meal, and do so without noticeable personality changes, cold hands and feet, or signs of tremendous stress. This shows great adaptability, a quality that no Ninja could survive without possessing.

Finally, we should talk a little bit about physical training as well. By that I mean exercise. You may be under the impression that this Food Ninja, eating every bite of decadent food that he or she desires, must need to exercise a lot to keep from getting fat. Sigh. That's not true. In fact, even if your kid hangs out in his pajamas all day doing nothing, you should note incredible physical energy expenditure through fidgeting—known in obesity research as non-exercise physical activity (NEPA). If Emily just had lighter bones she would fly away just reading a book. She's always flapping her arms and legs and bouncing around with comical vigor.

Having said that, physical activity is extremely important for humans of all ages. The problem is that we often approach physical movement with the wrong psychology in place—doing it to burn calories, lose weight, build muscle, or even be healthy. Exercise is not a necessary evil or a means to an end. Make it a chore to obtain something else that you want and it will always be a lot less enjoyable than it should be, and be something you are more likely to quit at some point.

Exercise itself improves quality of life. A day doing something physically is better than a day doing nothing physically. The reason to exercise is to keep your life from sucking. Any other benefits you notice are just nice perks.

Switching gears a little bit here, think of a dog. A dog, if nothing stimulating is going on, will just lay around and nap most of the day like a lump of crap. It's depressing just watching him. And the dog is always ALWAYS up for going out and doing some exercise. This is pure instinct. When relying on instinct with no psychological interference, humans would always be eager to go play. But our world is filled with psychological interference because we are such cerebral creatures. Books, television,

YouTube, the internet, video games—the list of things that keep us a lot more sedentary than we would otherwise be without these mental stimuli goes on and on. A television can keep us immobile for hours, nearly motionless. Try to sit in a chair and stare at the wall without moving for an entire day. You can't do it. Without a mental babysitter (electronic device), you want to get up and move around and do something.

As a parent, if you want a true Ninja Master kid, it is up to you to create an exciting exercise environment for your child. I'm not asking you to take away all electronics. This book is about preparing a child for reality, not closing your eyes and wishing it away. But do some stuff with your kids. Buy some weights. Go on walks. Get a trampoline in the back yard. Put them in gymnastics and dance. Take them to the pool. Go hiking with them. They will surprise you. And your quality of life will improve by engaging in all that stuff, too.

Easier said than done at times, but try. I'm as big of an electronics zombie as the next person, and I suffer some negative consequences for it (more stiffness, aches and pains, poor fitness, sleep loss), but you can be confident that my days of glaring into a computer screen for 10 hours a day are numbered.

And don't you dare call it "exercise" in front of your Ninja. Just call it "fun." Don't let little Ninjas think for a moment that they are doing it for a better body, better flexibility and agility, a leaner midsection, or to burn off the doughnuts. Physical activity is one of the greatest quality of life enhancers on the planet in a well-fed, metabolically-healthy person. And humans have an inner drive to get better at things, be it skateboarding or skiing or pull-ups or what have you. Give them that pleasure. They will reap health rewards for a lifetime if you don't push them too hard, but allow them to develop an incredible, instinctual fondness for that which is not sitting around on thy ass.

Put all these pieces together, and folks, you've got yourself a true, modern, Ninja Warrior.

CONCLUSION

You're right, this book is short. Damn it I hate it when you're right! I kill! I kill! I kill!

Other books about feeding kids are looonnggg. They are full of recipes fit for a rabbit and strange concoctions containing vile substances like raw beef liver. They are filled with cheesy games (part skim of course) and songs about vegetables and other unsuitable food. They are backed with lots of really relevant studies showing that 55 year olds in Norway had lower triglycerides after eating more vegetables for two weeks. Incontrovertible proof that forcing your child to eat broccoli will make her totally immune to disease until the ripe age of 120.

Listen, it's simple. You just need to get out of the way and let nature take over for the most part. If you feel confused after reading this and don't know what to do now, that's perfect. Do nothing. It's better than doing something in most cases. I mean that with the utmost sincerity. And I mean that with even more sincerity for those who will question this approach when their child appears to fall off the wagon and get chubby immediately upon being able to finally eat. That's all part of the process, too. Please trust it. For you, and for the long-term physical and psychological health of your child.

As a concise summary, following a brief goodbye is a top 10 list of important takeaways from this book. Thank you for reading and don't brush this book aside too quickly. If you think this wasn't well-researched, that I lack expertise in this area, or that I am unaware of so-and-so's research showing blah blah blah… You're wrong on all accounts. Play around with these ideas before casting judgment based on some seemingly impressive book you read. Yeah, I read it, too, and I bought into it for a while. It came up short. All health and nutrition ideas get incinerated when exposed to instinct and the metabolic flame. If you found yourself shocked and appalled at what you've read here and are shaking your head in aggressive disagreement, that's okay. But remember this book. At some point in your weird eating and dictatorial parenting career this book will start to make a lot more sense than it may now. And when it does, remember to bow to your sensei. BOW to your sensei!

1. Metabolic rate is the primary priority to focus on above all other health factors for your child's health status in the modern world.

2. Metabolic rate is optimized by keeping calorie intake high, getting lots of sleep, keeping stress levels low, and minimizing linoleic and arachidonic acids—two types of polyunsaturated fatty acids.

3. Pre-pregnancy, prenatal, and postnatal diet of a mother should be high in calories, featuring lots of pleasure foods, and low in polyunsaturated fat (LA and AA).

4. Urine should be yellow. Never clear.

5. The primary determinant of a child's calorie intake will be the palatability, calorie-density, and variety of a child's diet. Meals that combine starch, sugar, salt, and saturated fat usually provide the greatest appetite stimulus.

6. Kids should be able to eat whatever they want, whenever they want, and get in tune with their instinctual energy-regulating programming.

7. Kids shouldn't be pressured to eat more or less, or eat "x" while avoiding "y" or even eat something "in moderation." There are no "treats." Just food. Neutrality is the single-most important factor in the psychology of eating.

8. Some kids may not be able to just eat whatever. That may make them sick. As a parent, you should observe carefully and do the best you can without turning power over to someone who doesn't have any intimate knowledge of your child. But you should first attempt to train your child to be a Food Ninja with a 100% effort before resorting to grueling dietary omissions.

9. All of your efforts to make your child healthy should get results. If the results are not there (the items on the Metabolism Report Card), make some subtle changes.

10. A child should be presented with an interesting physical environment to foster physical fitness, strength, agility, and overall quality of life.

REFERENCES

Books

Bacon, Linda. *Health at Every Size*. Benbella Books: Dallas, TX, 2008.

Barnes, Broda. *Hypothyroidism: The Unsuspecting Illness*. Harper and Row: New York, NY, 1976.

Barnes, Broda. *Solved: The Riddle of Heart Attacks*. Robinson Press: Fort Collins, CO, 1976.

Barnes, Broda. *Hope for Hypoglycemia*. Robinson Press: Fort Collins, CO, 1978.

Bieler, Henry. *Food is Your Best Medicine*. Random House: New York, NY, 1965.

Brownstein, David. *Overcoming Thyroid Disorders*. Medical Alternative Press: West Bloomfield, MI, 2008.

Campos, Paul. *The Obesity Myth*. Gotham Books: New York, NY, 2004.

Chilton, Floyd H. *Inflammation Nation*. Fireside: New York, NY, 2007.

Keys, Ancel et al. *The Biology of Human Starvation*. The University of Minnesota Press: Minneapolis, MN, 1950.

Kharrazian, Datis. *Why Do I Still Have Thyroid Symptoms?* Morgan James Publishing: Garden City, NY, 2010.

Kolata, Gina. *Rethinking Thin*. Farrar, Straus and Giroux: New York, NY, 2007.

Langer, Stephen E. and James F. Scheer. *Solved: The Riddle of Illness*. McGraw Hill: New York, NY, 2006.

Martin, Courtney E. *Perfect Girls, Starving Daughters*. Free Press: New York, NY, 2007.

Murray, Michael. *The Encyclopedia of Healing Foods.* Atria Books: New York, NY, 2005.

Peat, Ray. *Progesterone in Orthomolecular Medicine.* Raymond Peat: Eugene, OR, 1993.

Peat, Ray. *Generative Energy.* Raymond Peat: Eugene, OR, 1994.

Peat, Ray. *Nutrition for Women.* Raymond Peat: Eugene, OR, 1993.

Peat, Ray. *Mind and Tissue.* Raymond Peat: Eugene, OR, 1993.

Peat, Ray. *From PMS to Menopause.* Raymond Peat: Eugene, OR, 1993.

Pool, Robert. *Fat: Fighting the Obesity Epidemic.* Oxford University Press: New York, NY, 2001.

Rooney, Ric. *Secrets of a Professional Dieter* (eBook). www.PhysiqueTransformation.com

Ross, Julia. *The Diet Cure.* Penguin Books: New York, NY, 1999.

Schwartz, Bob. *Diets Don't Work!* Breakthrough Publishing: Houston, TX, 1982.

Sears, Barry. *The Age-Free Zone.* Regan Books: New York, NY, 1999.

Sears, Barry. *The Anti-Inflammation Zone.* Collins: New York, NY, 2005.

Sears, Barry. *Toxic Fat.* Thomas Nelson Inc, 2008.

Shell, Ellen Ruppel. *The Hungry Gene.* Atlantic Monthly Press: New York, NY, 2002.

Starr, Mark. *Hypothyroidism Type II.* Mark Starr Trust: Columbia, MO, 2005.

Tribole, Evelyn and Elyse Resch. *Intuitive Eating.* St. Martin's Press: New York, NY, 1995.

Kohn, Alfie. *Punished By Rewards.*

Roth, Geneen. *When Food is Love.*

Studies

Linoleic and Arachidonic Acids
Linoleic acid content of breast milk and childhood obesity:
Ailhaud, Gérard. Florence Massiera , Pierre Weill, Philippe Legrand, Jean-Marc Alessandri, Philippe Guesnet. *Temporal changes in dietary fats: Role of n-6 polyunsaturated fatty acids in excessive adipose tissue development and relationship to obesity.* Progress in Lipid Research 45 (2006) 203–236.
http://www.tradilin.ch/downloads/docs/2006,%20Progress%20in%20Lipid%20Research,%20Temporal%20changes%20in%20dietary%20fats....Ailhaud.pdf

Sampling of references showing the myriad negative effects of Polyunsaturated fatty acids (PUFA), including linoleic and arachidonic acids. Studies compiled and posted at the website www.pranarupa.wordpress.com :

Ayre KJ, Hulbert AJ (1997), *Dietary fatty acid profile affects endurance in rats*, Lipids, 32(12), pp. 1265-1270.

Bajra G, (2004), *Free radicals and aging*, Trends Neurosci, 27(10), pp. 595-600.
Borkman M, Chisholm DJ, Furler SM, Storlien LH, Kraegen EW, Simons LA, Chesterman CN, (1989), *Effects of fish oil supplementation on glucose and lipid metabolism in NIDDM*, Diabetes, 38(10), pp. 1314-1319.

Brasky TM, Till C, White E, Neuhouser ML, Song X, Goodman P, Thompson IM, King IB, AlbanesD, Kristal AR, (2011), *Serum Phospholipid Fatty Acids and prostate cancer risk: results from the prostate cancer prevention trial*, Am J. Epidemiol, doi: 10.1093/aje/kwr027.

Burr GO, and Beber AJ, (1934), *Metabolism studies with rats suffering from fat deficiency*, Exp Biol Med, 31(8), pp. 911-912.

Cardosso CR, Souza MA, Ferro EA, Favoretto S Jr, Pena JD, (2004), *Influence of topical administration of n-3 and n-6 essential and n-9 nonessential fatty acids on the healing of cutaneous wounds*, Wound Repair Regen, 12(2), pp. 235-243.

Chan PH, and Fishman RA, (1980), *Transient formation of superoxide radicals in polyunsaturated fatty acid-induced brain swelling*, J Neurochem, 35(4), pp. 1004-1007.

Clarke SD, and Hembree J, (1990), *Inhibition of triiodothyronine's induction of rat liver lipogenic enzymes by dietary fat*, J Nutr, 120(6), pp. 625-630.

Da Silva LA, De Marcucci OL, Kuhnle ZR, (1993), *Dietary polyunsaturated fats suppress the high-sucrose-induced increase of rat liver pyruvate dehydrogenase*, Biochim Biophys Acta, 69(2), pp. 126-134.

Felton CV, Crook D, Davies MJ, Olivier MF, (1994), *Dietary polyunsaturated fatty acids and composition of human aortic plaques*, Lancet, 344(8931), pp. 1195-1196.

Garza LA, Liu Y, Yang Z, Alagesan B, Lawson JA, Norberg SM, Loy DE, Zhao T, Blatt HB, Stanton DC, Carrasco L, Ahluwalia G, Fischer SM, FitzGerald GA, Cotsarelis G, (2012), *Prostaglandin D2 inhibits hair growth and is elevated in bald scalp of men with androgenic alopecia*, Sci Transl Med, 4(126).

Griffini P, Fehres O, Klieverik L, Vogels IM, Tigchelaar W, Smorenburg SM, Van Noorden CJ, (1998), *Dietary omega-3 polyunsaturated fatty acids promote colon carcinoma metastasis in rat liver*, Cancer Res, 58(15), pp. 3312-3319.

Harman D, Hendricks S, Eddy DE, Seibold J, (1976), *Free radical theory of aging: effect of dietary fat on central nervous system function*, J Am Geriatr Soc, 24(7), pp. 301-307.

Humphries KM, Yoo Y, Szweda LI, (1998), *Inhibition of NADH-linked mitochondrial respiration by 4-hydroxy-2-nonenal*, Biochemistry, 37(2), pp. 552-557.

Ip C, Carter CA, Ip MM, (1985), *Requirement of essential fatty acid for mammary tumorigenesis in the rat*, Cancer Res, 45(5), pp. 1997-2001.

Kjaer MA, Todorcevic M, Torsten BE, Vegusdal A, Ruyter B, (2008), *Dietary n-3 HUFA affects mitochondrial fatty acid beta-oxidation capacity and susceptibility to oxidative stress in Atlantic salmon*, Lipids, 43(9), pp. 813-827.

Kunkel HO, and Williams JN Jr, (1951), *The effects of fat deficiency upon enzyme activity in the rat*, J Biol Chem, 189(2), pp. 755-761.

Ling PR, Malkan A, Le HD, Puder M, Bistrian BR, (2012), *Arachidonic acid and docosahexaenoic acid supplemented to an essential fatty acid-deficient diet alters the response to endotoxin in rats*, Metabolism, 61(3), pp. 395-406.

McFate T, Mohyeldin A, Lu H, Thakar J, Henriques J, Halim ND, Wu H, Schell MJ, Tsang TM, Teahan O, Zhou S, Califano JA, Jeoung NH, Harris RA, Verma A, (2008), *Pyruvate dehydrogenase complex activity controls metabolic and malignant phenotype in cancer cells*, J Biol Chem, 283(33), pp. 22700-22708.
Nanji AA, and French SW, (1986), *Dietary factors and alcoholic liver cirrhosis*, Alcohol Clin Exp Res, 10(3), pp. 271-273.

Nanji AA, Jokelainen K, Tipoe GL, Rahemtulla A, Dannenberg AJ, (2001), *Dietary saturated fatty acids reverse inflammatory and fibrotic changes in rat liver despite continued ethanol administration*, J Pharmacol Exp Ther, 299(2), pp. 638-644.

Nourooz-Zadeh J, and Pereira P, (1999), *Age-related accumulation of free polyunsaturated fatty acids in human retina*, Opthalmic Res, 31(4), pp. 273-279.

Picklo MJ, and Montine TJ, (2001), *Acrolein inhibits respiration in isolated brain mitochondria*, Biochim Biophys Acta, 1535(2), pp. 145-152.

Rafael J, Patzelt J, Elmadfa I, (1988), *Effect of dietary linoleic acid and essential fatty acid deficiency on resting metabolism, nonshivering thermogenesis and brown adipose tissue in the rat*, J Nutr, 118(5), pp. 627-632.

Roberts LJ, Montine TJ, Markesbery WR, Tapper AR, Hardy P, Chemtob S, Dettbarn WD, Morrow JD, (1998), *Formation of isoprostane-like compounds (neuroprostanes) in vivo from docosahexaenoic acid*, J Biol Chem, 273(22), pp. 13605-13612.

Solfrizzi V, D'Introno A, Colacicco AM, Capsurso C, Palasciano R, Capurso S, Torres F, Capurso A, Panza F, (2005) *Unsaturated fatty acids intake and all-causes mortality: a 8.5-year follow-up of the Italian longitudinal study on aging*, Exp Gerontl, 40(4), pp. 335-343.

Tamburini I, Quartacci MF, Izzo R, Bergamini E, (2004), *Effects of dietary restriction on age-related changes in the phospholipid fatty acid composition of various rat tissues*, Aging Clin Exp Res, 16(6), pp. 425-431.

Wolf RB, (1982) *Effect of temperature on soybean seed constituents*, J Am Oil Chem Soc, 59: 230-2.
Wolfe RR, Martini WZ, Irtun O, Hawkins HK, Barrow RE, (2002), *Dietary fat composition alters pulmonary function in pigs*, Nutrition, 18(7-8), pp. 647-653.

Yoshida H, Soh H, Sando K, Wasa M, Takagi Y, Okada A, (2003), *Beneficial effects of n-9 eicosatrienoic acid on experimental bowel lesions*, Surg Today, 33(8), pp. 600-605.

Intuitive Eating Studies
The following studies show the health and body composition effects of eating in a more instinctive way. Several studies apply to children and younger people specifically. Compiled by authors of the book *Intuitive Eating* by Evelyn Tribole and Elyse Resch at www.intuitiveeating.com :

2013 Studies
Herbert BL, Blechert J, Hautzinger M, Matthias E., Herbert C.. (2013). *Intuitive eating is associated with interoceptive sensitivity. Effects on body mass index.* Appetite, 70(Nov):22–30.

Denny KN, Loth K, Eisenberg ME, Neumark-Sztainer D (2013). *Intuitive eating in young adults. Who is doing it, and how is it related to disordered eating behaviors?* Appetite.Jan;60(1):13-9.

Tylka TL, & Kroon Van Diest AM. (2013) *The Intuitive Eating Scale-2: Item refinement and psychometric evaluation with college women and men.* J Couns Psychol. Jan;60(1):137-53.

2012 Studies
Gast, J., Madanat H., & Nielson A. (2012). *Are Men More Intuitive When It Comes to Eating and Physical Activity?* Am J Mens Health, vol. 6 no. 2 164-17. Men scoring high on Hawks' Intuitive Eating scale, was associated with lower body mass index. Men placed value on being physically fit and healthy, rather than on an ideal weight.

Madden C.E., Leong, S.L., Gray A., and Horwath C.C. (2012). *Eating in response to hunger and satiety signals is related to BMI in a nationwide sample of 1601 mid-age New Zealand women.* Public Health Nutrition. Mar 23:1-8. [Epub ahead of print]. Women with high Intuitive Eating Scale (IES) scores had significantly lower body mass index, which suggests that people who eat in response to hunger and satiety cues, have unconditional permission to eat, and cope with feelings without food, are less likely to engage in eating behaviors that lead to weight gain.

2011 Studies
Augustus-Horvath CL and Tylka T. (2011) *The Acceptance Model of Intuitive Eating: A Comparison of Women in Emerging Adulthood, Early Adulthood, and Middle Adulthood.* J Counseling Psychology 2011 (Jan) 58:110-125. The acceptance model of intuitive eating posits that body acceptance by others helps women appreciate their body and resist adopting an observer's perspective of their body, which contribute to their eating intuitively/adaptively. We extended this model by integrating body mass index (BMI) into its structure and investigating it with emerging age, in adult women from ages 18–65 years old.

Heileson J.L., & R. Cole (2011). *Assessing Motivation for Eating and Intuitive Eating in Military Service Members.* Journal of the American Dietetic Association, 111 (9 Supplement), Page A26. Intuitive Eating was associated with lower body mass index levels in 100 active military troops.

Dockendorff, S. A., Petrie, T. A., Greenleaf, C., & Martin, S. (2011, August).*Intuitive Eating Scale for Adolescents: Factorial and construct validity.* Paper presented at the 119th annual American Psychological Association conference, Washington, DC. Tylka's Intuitive Eating scale was adopted for adolescents and Intuitive Eating was associated with health benefits including lower body mass index, without internalizing the thin ideal, positive mood, and greater life satisfaction.

Sarah H. Shouse S. J. & Nilsson, J. (2011). *Self-Silencing, Emotional Awareness, and Eating Behaviors in College Women.* Psychology of Women Quarterly, 35: 451-457. Expression of thoughts, feelings, or needs seems to be a critical aspect of healthy eating behaviors. The suppression of voice, combined with high levels of emotional awareness, may decrease trust of internal signals of hunger and satiation and disrupt Intuitive Eating. Intuitive eating is maximized when a woman has high levels of emotional awareness and low levels of self-silencing. Conversely, intuitive eating is disrupted.

Young, S. *Promoting healthy eating among college women: Effectiveness of an intuitive eating intervention.* Iowa State University, 2011, Dissertation 147 pages; AAT 3418683. This is the first experimental study to test the effectiveness of an intuitive eating intervention designed to increase adaptive eating practices and reduce eating disorder risk factors. Overall these results present empirical evidence that the intuitive eating model can be a promising approach to disordered eating prevention in a variety of service delivery modalities.

2010 Studies
Cole RE and Horacek T. *Effectiveness of the "My Body Knows When" Intuitive-eating Pilot Program.* Am J Health Behavior 2010; (May-June):286-297. The objective of this study was to evaluate the effectiveness of the "My Body Knows When" Intuitive Eating program tailored to assist Fort Drum military spouses in rejecting the dieting mentality. The intuitive-eating program was able to significantly transition participants away from a dieting mentality towards intuitive-eating lifestyle behaviors. Overall, Intuitive Eating is a holist approach to long-term healthy behavior change and would benefit from an extended support system to improve effectiveness.

Galloway A.T., Farrow, C.V., & Martz DM. (2010). *Retrospective Reports of Child Feeding Practices, Current Eating Behaviors, and BMI in College Students.* Behavior and Psychology (formerly Obesity), 18(7):1330-1335. Nearly 100 college-aged students and their parents completed retrospective questionnaires of parental feeding practices regarding the college students' childhood. The results showed that parental monitoring and restriction of food intake had a significant impact on their college student's body mass index, emotional eating, and Intuitive Eating Scale scores.

MacDougall EC. *An Examination of a Culturally Relevant Model of Intuitive Eating with African American College Women.* University of Akron, 2010. Dissertation 218 pages. The present study explores the model intuitive eating with African American college women. Results of the present study provide empirical support for several propositions underlying a model of intuitive eating that suggests several, but not all, model paths may extend and generalize to more diverse samples of women.

2008-2009 Studies
Mathieu J. *What Should You Know about Mindful and Intuitive Eating?* J Am Dietetic Assoc 2009;109(Dec):1982-1987.

Weigenberg, MJ. *Intuitive Eating Is Associated with Decreased Adiposity* (2009, Abstract).

Cole R & Horacek T. *Applying PRECEDE-PROCEED to Develop an Intuitive Eating Nondieting Approach to Weight Management Pilot Program.* J Nutrition Educ & Behavior.2009;41(Mar-Apr):120-126.

Mensinger JL. *Intuitive eating: A novel health promotion strategy for obese women.*[abstract] Nov 2009 Am Publ Health Assoc Conference.

Smitham LA. *Evaluating an Intuitive Eating Program for Binge Eating Disorder: A Benchmarking Study.* Univ Notre Dame Nov 2008.

2006-2007 Studies
Cole R & Horacek T. *Effectiveness of the "My Body Knows When" Intuitive Eating Non-Dieting Weight Management Pilot Program.*J Am Dietetic Assoc 2007;107(August Suppl):A90.

Tylka, Tracy L. *Development and psychometric evaluation of a measure of intuitive eating.*J Counseling Psych;2006. 53(2), Apr:226-240.

Avalos LC and Tylka T. *Exploring an acceptance model of intuitive eating with college women.*J Counseling Psych. Vol 53(4), Oct 2006, 486-497.

Hawks, ST et al. *The relationship between intuitive eating and health indicators among college women.* Am. J. Health Educ. 2006;26:322-324.

Tylka, T.L., & Wilcox, J.A. *Are intuitive eating and eating disorder symptomatology opposite poles of the same construct?* J of Counseling Psychology, 2006;53, 474-485.

Smith T and Hawks SR. *Intuitive Eating, Diet Composition, and the Meaning of Food in Healthy Weight Promotion.* Am J Health Educ 2006;May-June;37(3):130-136..

Intuitive Eating and Healthy Weight Promotion. AJHE, 2006

2004-2005 Studies
Bacon L. *Size Acceptance and Intuitive Eating Improve Health in Obese Female Chronic Dieters.* J Am Dietetic Assoc.2005;105:929-936.

Hawks S et al. *Relationship Between Intuitive Eating and Health Indicators Among College Women.* Am J Health Ed 2005:Nov-Dec;36(6):331-336

Hawks, SR. *The Intuitive Eating Validation Scale: preliminary validation.* Am. J. Health Educ. 2004;35:26-35.

Hawks, SR e. *Intuitive eating and the nutrition transition in Asia.* Asia Pac J Clin Nutr. 2004;13(2):194-203.

More Studies Related to Intuitive Eating
Bacon L and Aphramor L. *Weight Science: Evaluating the Evidence for a Paradigm Shift.* [2011]. Nutrition Journal, January. 10:9. http://bit.ly/f4CKOK .
Ciampolini M et al., *Sustained Self-Regulation of Energy Intake: Initial Hunger Improves Insulin Sensitivity,* Journal of Nutrition and Metabolism, vol. 7 2010.

Ciampolini M et al. *Sustained self-regulation of energy intake. Loss of weight in overweight subjects. Maintenance of weight in normal-weight subjects,* Nutrition and Metabolism, vol. 7, article 4, 2010.

Ciampolini Mand R. Bianchi, *Training to estimate blood glucose and to form associations with initial hunger,* Nutrition and Metabolism, vol. 3, article 42, 2006.

Eneli et al. (2008). *The Trust Model: A Different Feeding Paradigm for Managing Childhood Obesity.Obesity.*2197-2204.

Field AE et al.(2003).*Relation Between Dieting and Weight Change Among Preadolescents and Adolescents*. Pediatrics, 112:900-906.

Mann, T. (2001).*Medicare's search for effective obesity treatments: Diets are not the answer*. Am. Psychologist, 62(3): 220-233.

Neumark-Sztainer D, Wall M, Guo J, Story M, Haines J, Eisenberg M. (2006). *Obesity, disordered eating, and eating disorders in a longitudinal study of adolescents: how do dieters fare five years later?* J Am Diet Assoc, 106(4):559-568.

K H Pietiläinen, S E Saarni, J Kaprio and A Rissanen (2011). *Does dieting make you fat? A twin study*. International Journal of Obesity.

Stice E et al. *An Effectiveness Trial of a Dissonance-Based Eating Disorder Prevention Program for High-Risk Adolescents Girls* J Consult Clin Psychol. 2009.October;77(5): 825–834. [Free Full Text.]

Shift from dieting decreases risk of obesity and eating disorders. JADA;2006 Apr;106:559-68.
Tomiyama, A. Janet, Mann, Traci, Vinas, Danielle, Hunger, Jeffrey M., DeJager, Jill, Taylor, Shelley E.*Low Calorie Dieting Increases Cortisol*. Psychosom Med. 2010 72: 357-364.

Yang Q. (2010).*Gain weight by "going diet?" Artificial sweeteners and the neurobiology of sugar cravings*.Yale J BIOLOGY MEDICINE, 83:01-108.

Websites

www.raypeat.com
www.andrewkimblog.com
www.dannyroddy.com
www.pranarupa.wordpress.com
www.junkfoodscience.blogspot.com
www.youreatopia.com
www.intuitiveeating.org
www.haescommunity.org
www.eastwesthealing.com
www.chiefrok.com/blog
www.billycraig.co.uk

About the Author

Matt Stone is an independent health researcher and author of 15 books on various health-related topics. He launched an independent investigation into health in 2005, and has since been exploring a wide range of health fields - from general physiology and nutrition to areas as diverse and specific as psychoneuroendocrinology. His investigation has yielded many great, practical insights and simple tips on how regular people can make substantial improvements in their health - for the purpose of both improving or eliminating specific health problems and preventing some of the most common ailments in the modern world. Most of his research has drawn him towards metabolic rate and how many basic functions (digestion, reproduction, aging, immunity, inflammation, sleep) perform better when metabolic rate is optimized.

Printed in Great Britain
by Amazon.co.uk, Ltd.,
Marston Gate.